T0132294

I AM READY TO LEARN MY ABC
AND
I AM READY TO LEARN NUMBERS 1 TO 10
WITH YOU

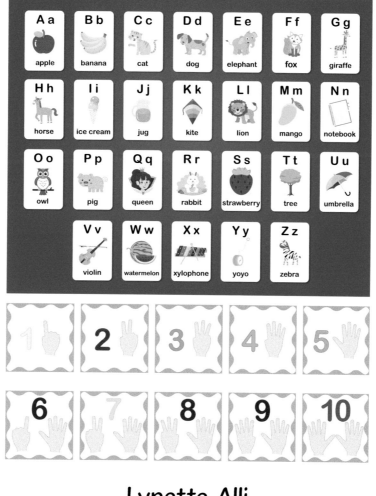

Lynette Alli

To order additional copies of this book, contact:
Xlibris
844-714-8691
www.Xlibris.com
Orders@Xlibris.com

ISBN: Softcover   978-1-6641-4076-9
        EBook   978-1-6641-4075-2

Print information available on the last page

Rev. date: 11/25/2020

Children learn by seeing, hearing and touching.

This book is an introduction to the alphabet, and numbers.

This book will prepare young children to
read, learn numbers, and write.

Also, its readiness for school.

I am ready to learn my ABC,
and numbers with you.

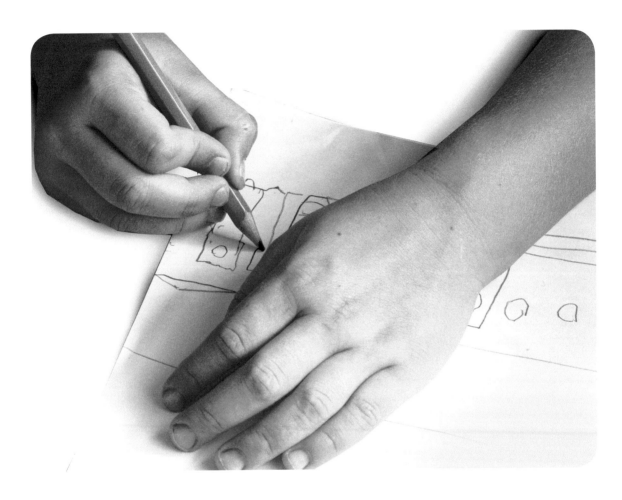

I am ready to learn my ABC
and
I am ready to learn numbers 1 to 10
with you.

A is for the alphabet.
My name starts with letter_____ .
Letters make up words, like my name and
Your name

Some words I know are
Happy birthday, milk, and cookie.

Some numbers I know are 1, 2, and 3.

Words I like to say are Mom, Dad, and I love you.

I love to say numbers like 1, 2, and 3.

Some words I hear every day, say please, say thank you.

Great work.

I see many letters and words

I see numbers 1, 2, 3, and more numbers.

I know ABC songs and number songs.

I like to sing ABC songs and number songs 1, 2, 3.

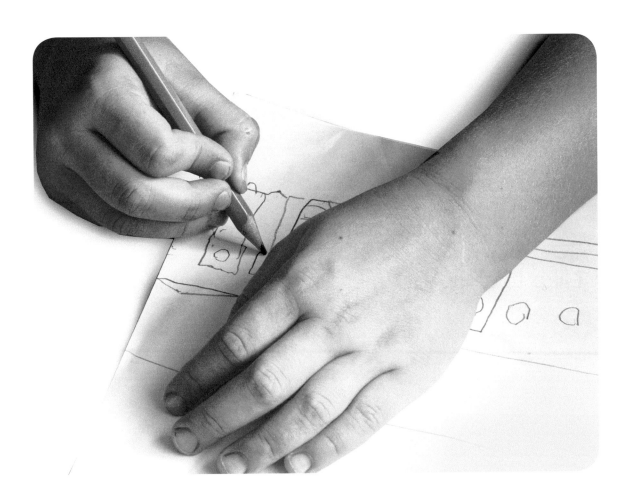

I am ready to know more about letters and words.

I am ready to learn more about numbers and words.

Me and you, letters, words, and numbers.

The Alphabet

A a apple	B b banana	C c cat	D d dog	E e elephant	F f fox	G g giraffe
H h horse	I i ice cream	J j jug	K k kite	L l lion	M m mango	N n notebook
O o owl	P p pig	Q q queen	R r rabbit	S s strawberry	T t tree	U u umbrella
V v violin	W w watermelon	X x xylophone	Y y yoyo	Z z zebra		

I know my ABC and my ABC words.

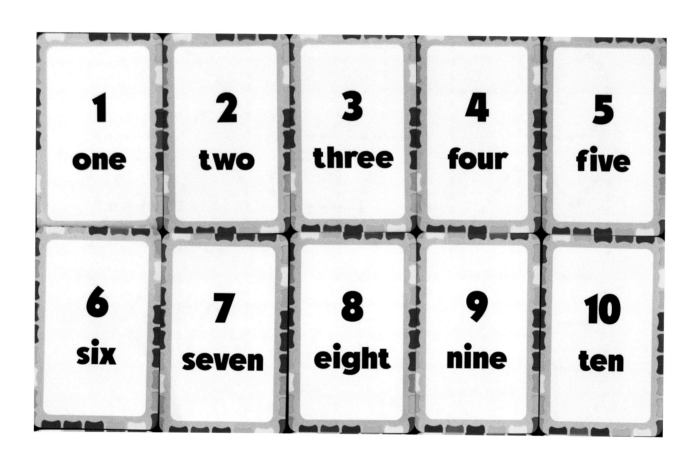

I know my numbers and words from one to ten.

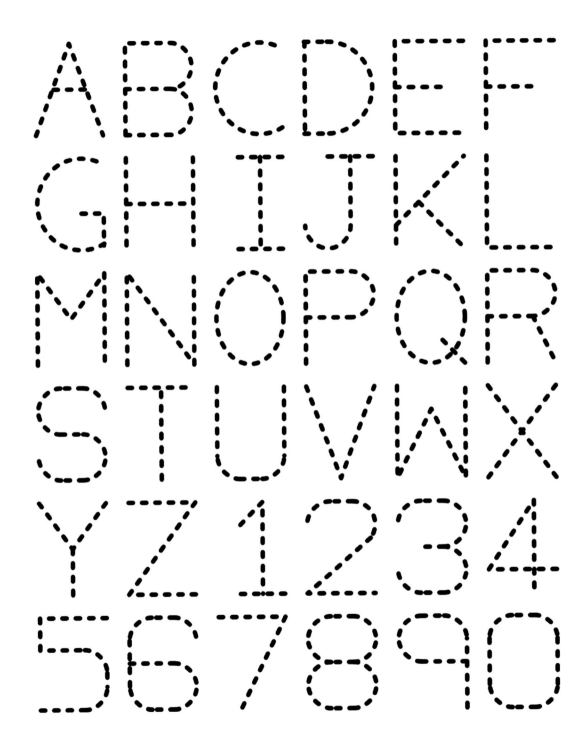

I can trace my ABC letters.

I can trace my numbers.

School Bus

Now I am ready to go to school.

Printed in the United States
By Bookmasters